West Palm Beach, Florida

MICHELLE WALKER

ISBN: 978-1-954755-08-6

Published by:
Restoration of the Breach without Borders
133 45th Street, Building A7
West Palm Beach, Florida 33407
restorativeauthor@gmail.com
Tele: (561) 388-2949

EBook Cover Design by:
Tevaughn Brown
tbartgraphics@gmail.com

Editing done by:
Melisha Bartley-Ankle
melbarxtd@yahoo.com

Formatting and Publishing done by:
Sherene Morrison
Publisher.20@aol.com

TABLE OF CONTENTS

DEDICATION

Dedicated to and in living memory of my Mom, Miss Cynthia lodge.

ACKNOWLEDGEMENTS

I'd like to acknowledge:

Mr Eli Smith who believed in me and sponsored this book. Much thanks Eli!

My Daughters Talena and Ashanti who are always in my corner cheering me on. I love you my daughters.

God, the Father who gave me the talent to write.

My Mom who always believed in me and dreamt that one day I'd publish a book of poetry. You will always be in my heart.

Mr Osbourne Southerland, affectionately called daddy, who encouraged and made me see how special my gift was.

Dr Alex Tracey of Online Medics for his moral and technical support. Sir you are always ready and willing to assist in anyway needed. I thank you.

I'd like to thank a very special person, Mr Cedric Demetrius, who showed me that love is stronger than Pain and regret. He gave my heart another chance and made me love again, and put colours to my words. Thank You CJ. I love you.

ENDORSEMENT

I met Michelle Walker while she was a brilliant starry eyed, young teenager. I was immediately struck with her intelligence, powers of analysis and expressive, articulate elocution. She possessed a depth and maturity that was way beyond her years. The influence of a stridently Christian, insightful, innovative mother who, without the aid of conventional academia was employed by a multinational company and functioned expertly in the capacity of auditor. This mother spent Sabbath (Saturday) mornings in church services, lunch less noons in the vestry securing the institution's finances and afternoons in a local prison offering hope and opportunity to the incarcerated. Can you imagine a single mother providing (temporary) domicile for a converted prisoner who wanted to go back to school? Such was the mother of poet Michelle Walker. There was one major crisis and this may be the most decisive factor in the depth and breadth of this outstanding daughter: Early in her earthly sojourn, Michelle lost her father; a dad she dearly loved... a father who used to comb her hair.... She has not seen him for decades.....but has forgiven and loves him with all her heart. Could this factor help to inspire her exceptional love for the rejected, dejected despised, downtrodden and all kinds of creatures belonging to the animal kingdom? It is these and many other factors (including the fact that she shared her mother's womb with a twin brother whose personal welfare created the conditions for our first meeting that have helped to make Ms Walker the prolific writer she is. She has been a teacher of the deaf, a lover of music (focusing on the guitar) driver of huge utility vehicles, an experienced wife and devoted mother.

Drink deeply from the fount of her life.

-Osbourne Sutherland
Guidance Counsellor (Retired)

INTRODUCTION

There are times when there are just no words to describe how we are feeling. We do not even know that someone has been there before who was able to find the right words and put them on paper.

These poems are from different times in my life, different situations and circumstances that I know people can attest to.

After a failed marriage and the victim of a Narcissist relationship, I was forced to put me first...to fall in love with me. Some of these poems show my journey into self-actualization, my levelling up. Sometimes pain can be a good medicine because it propels you into a you, you never knew existed. Pain had become my voice and when I found my voice I could not stop writing. Now I write about everything, happiness, falling in love, heartbreak, everything. I am sure there is something in here for you. Read and enjoy.

SECTION ONE: LIFE

This speaks to our everyday challenges, heart break, joy, disappointments and evolution to a higher self, victory over others as well as victory over ourselves which can prove to be our worst enemies.

A SINNER'S PRAYER

Lord do you understand what goes on inside this mind of mine?
Please enlighten me with an answer divine
I get so confused Lord, between my mind and my person. Each time I seek to do right my actions only worsen.
If you think I have a chance to be what you know I can be,
Then dear Lord, please show this to me.
If you can reach down and touch this heart of mine,
Then do so Lord and to my prayers thy ears incline...
And Lord please let me be the best of what you have made.
Let me never thy standards degrade.
May each morning I awake, greet you with a smile
With such probity and earnest like a little child.
As I depart, with all my heart,
I hope my prayers you've heard
Yes Lord each and every word
Until I speak to you again,
Dear Lord continue being my best friend.
Amen.

AGAIN

They say time heals a broken heart,
So what about mine?
When everyone else is happy, why am I always crying?
God, does my heart have a special
Room that I don't know about?
Does this flickering light of pain and hurt ever at all go out?
Where does all the pain go when you don't know what to do with it?
I wish I could, yes, I think I will really quit
Why do you feel I have to hang in there?
Do I not get some breathing space?
I am growing tired now, exhausted and totally weary.
I will have to retire now for even my limbs are dreary.
Now, so sad and all hope in vain.
I'm so empty… again and again.

BETRAYED

You say you are my friend but yet you lie.
Never considering the things you say, always making me cry
Never saw through you, so opaque as wood.
Little did I know you were up to no good.
Took me too long to see the venomous poison slithering through your veins.
Now that I have discovered this,
My heart surely pains.
Be careful for life is full of tricks and the raw deals.
One day you will surely know how it truly feels.
You may just get the same hand you dished out,
Then you will discover what betrayal is all about.
So never you be the points of a fork that dish as it will and dash as they may,
For life is full of sharp edges that may come your way some day.
Always be as good a friend as you can be,
That is all life expects of you and me.

BLUE FLAME

I am a blue flame so deep and bright.
All of your senses to ignite.
With a passion of fire,
Igniting your desire.
With words so deep,
Sweeping you off your feet.
I am a blue flame provoking your inner man,
Trying to make you understand.
Like fire and ice,
Quite often to splice,
A mix of the two…
That is all me, oh yes its true.
I am a blue flame again and again,
Let there be fires of rain,
Pouring out without measure.
Finding out the treasure,
That lies in my soul,
Always to make me whole.
I am a blue flame, with soul on fire.
With a bold in me no one can hire...
So I will employ,
Life to enjoy.
In the heat of it all,
The blue deep so tall.
Flame in my eyes reaching for the stars.
Leaving everything behind, shaking off the scars.
Passion burning, making steps higher,
Blue depths of yearning, lighting me on fire.
I'm at the bottom of the sea
With depths as deep as can be,
But all that I need still remains,
In me, I will fire up the flame.

GRAND MOMMY

As I lay in my little space listening to my mommy talk about you,
I am wondering when I enter your world,
Without you grand mommy, what would mommy do?
I like being here in my warm little space.
But I would give it up all in a second, just to see you face to face.
Mommy writes whenever she can. I am so happy, I dance and wave my hands.
Grand mommy, thanks for filling my world with joy and delight.
I cannot wait for my tiny eyes
To behold your beautiful sight.
I hope yours is the first face I will see
Yes, you my beautiful grand mommy.

GOODBYE...THE LETTER

To be loved or to be missed, the art of leaving trails of you...
Bits and pieces of your soul.
As I say goodbye to sentiments,
Monuments of myself embedded in the fabric of time.
I seal the hurt of a thousand songs.
With lost melodies, lost tunes
Nothingness holds me dear...
Goodbye,
Those tears you will shed
Only footsteps to the horizon of new beginnings, now and hereafter.
Joining the two, the now and the never will be, a reckoning of what ifs and whys
The empty, so full of unforgiveness and never minds.
Only seeking to parallel the hurt of avalanched tears and sorrows....
Goodbye,
In a bit, time frolicks away out of our hands.
Carefree, without a thought of obligation or honour to those left behind.
I say goodbye to you and goodbye to me.
Goodbye to every moleculic presence.... goodbye.

HOW COULD IT BE?

How could it be?
Started so innocently,
You pronounced a kiss upon my lips,
With your arms around my hips.
Then you looked into my eyes,
Tearing away my disguise,
Dispelling all the lies,
I tell myself.
You are the shade under which I rest,
As I lay my weary head upon your chest.
And feel the exchange of our souls,
Wanting to me us whole
How could it be?
So mysteriously,
I gave you the key to my heart
Though torn apart
And ripped asunder,
By lightning and thunder.
Yet you knew the right words to say
Each day,
Tearing down the walls I worked too hard to build,
Giving me quite a thrill.
To see my walls come tumbling down,
Will not even make a sound.
How could it be?
Unequivocally,
You won where others failed
To get my heart out on bail.
I melt like wax in your arms
With effortless charm.
I like the way you rub my feet
Oh yes, it's such a treat.
You run your fingers through my hair,

As if you really care
And then you ask if I’m ok,
If you see my thoughts astray.
When I get home, my food you'd prepare,
Shows me how much you truly care.
All this coming I didn't see,
I ask myself
How could it be?
Tell me, how could it be?

HAVE YOU SEEN HER?

Could have sworn I left her here yesterday.
She wore a cumbersome smile.
Her soul receding into nothingness.
Nonchalant, she stood, unwilling to fight.
Estranged from her Lord and all she knew.
Where is she?
She wore a garment of duplicity. She reserved the rights to tearfulness and oh such mendacity as she hides from herself disowning all she is, reverting to a self she never knew.
Have you seen her?
Has she retired to weep some more,
Over dreams abandoned and unrealized?
In compliance with procrastination, the murderer of dreams and the facilitator
Of tyranny,
Wait....
Who is this?
A being of illumination!
She resembles the one I seek yet... Something is afoot.
Such apathy for sorrow,
Withdrawing from the deal to be barren of happiness.
Manipulating her way through murky waters, she steps higher, walks taller!
She looks like her… but her countenance on fire! Flamed filled eyes
As she burns with a passion for life and elevations of the highest.
Avalanching any weight attempting to keep her back to regression of her former self.
Unaffected by the darts of the evil one, she moves only forward, reaping all she would sowed in the vineyard of hope.
Dreams on the horizon about to overflow,
Disrobed of disappointment she conquers.
She has claimed victory as her token and with pride, answer a question, asked.
"Yes, I have seen her, leaving her cocoon. She has become a butterfly, becoming all she was meant to be. Standing taller than any tree."

I DIED

I died a time or two from the darkness of the shadows that did me wrong.
I died and no one even knew the song unsung.
Emptiness to fill the void where holes are not few.
Hurts and pains, there is nothing that is true
I died to my sorrow of the last tomorrow
As I pay homage to the vacuum, a void left within,
Like moth to a flame there's a deeper sin.
So as I die to a self-long forgotten, each letter of every word,
I also die to sorrow, every note unheard.

I AM

No one, no one can take me away from me.
I am and will be what I want to be.
I am an individual with all my earthly right.
I have the right to do what I want to do,
Let me fight my own fight.
Do not dictate to me or tell me what you think,
You think in this chain, I am the weakest link.
No one is a part of me, but me myself.
You cannot take my heart
And put on a shelf.
I am beautiful inside and out.
You cannot with your negative vibes make me doubt,
All that is good and beautiful within.
All your evil desires cannot make me sin.
You see my mind you cannot control at all.
My strength and faith, cannot cause to fall.
If you cannot accept me for who I am,
Then away with you, for still I shall stand...
Cause no one, no one can take me away from me.
I am ,and will be what I want to be.

INSIDE OF ME

There is sadness in my soul today,
For whatever come what may.
An emptiness, a need to belong.
A need to hurt, to right a wrong.
There is hunger in my soul today.
What can satisfy me this day?
A crave.. A longing to achieve,
Does anyone in me believe?
There is conflict in my soul today.
Be still my heart, I pray.
A war, a battle of the mind.
Mutiny of the heart, will I ever peace find?

JUST FOR YOU

It is great the way I feel about you
Having driven away my dark clouds,
My skies are forever blue.
You are nice to be with and I really like your smile.
Spending quiet evenings with you is simply worth the while.
I hope this friendship of ours will blossom and bloom,
Like the beautiful flowers in the month of June.
May we learn more and more about each other with each passing day,
And learn to deal with the trials that may come our way.

INTROSPECTION

As I dissect and introspect I am left to reflect,
On things I hold dear, no sorrow no fear.
As I implore, to restore a heart that has no cure,
For the tumultuous heartbreak,
For my sake cannot take fake.....
People.
Tribalism of the heart, so torn apart.
As I digress and regress with finesse,
Often blessed
With,
Prolific thoughts often quite profligate to the imaginings a song unsung, for so long, not yet begun.
So here I admonish, yet to demolish,
Those affixed with negativity no positivity nor eccentricity
For,
A beauty so rare and grand, cannot understand it is a plan,
So infinite please expedite with all your might so out of sight some people that might,
Attach themselves to greatness untold,
From days of old, yet so bold.
To have and to hold but not
Cherish,
Cause I perish from the hellish,
From blind with no peace of... Mind.

IT'S OVER

I so want to tell you it is over, but fear you will shatter like glass.
So abstruse are my feelings towards you, like green on grass.
You've held heart a hostage too long,
It's time for me to put back music to that lifeless song.
I'm taking me from you, no cobwebs over my eyes.
I'm standing taller, seeing over your lies.
A vixen in me have you awakened,
I see you were simply mistaken.
Taking my sweetness for weakness,
Misunderstanding my finesse.
It's plain to see you mistook diamond for glass.
So much so, your time has passed.

LOOK AT YOUUUUU

Girl me jus love how yuh step up yuh ting,
Cause life ain't no ring ding.
Pan all a de haters dem pop style.
An pon yuh face put a smile.
Weh dem did deh wen all night u a wash bus?
Weh dem did deh when no sleep was a mus?
But yuh pride did taller dan the mountain top.
Climbing the success ladder , yuh never stop.
Gallang a school yaah me fren,
Get yuh qualifications pon the haters dem.
Now yuh move from the bus wash inna a de office,
Da place deh, a nuh fi novice.
Ambition taller dan mount everest
Cause you strive for only the best.
Girl me proud a yuh caaa done.
Yuh smile is brighter dan the sun.
Me know fi yuh de sky a de limit,
An me see a bright future wid yuh inna it.
Gallang an pap style pan dem me fren!
Dem tink dis is the end.
See deh now yuh publish a book,
An if yuh did pon me face look,
Yuh woulda see eye wata like river nile
A run dung me face, wid a smile.
Gwaaan yaah me fren me deh yah a watch yuh journey ahead.
When yuh get famous me a siddung pon me bed,
An call everybody me know
An dem yuh pitcha show.
"Yes me dear me know har long time, she is a big friend a mine."
Brag and boast bout yuh fame
An tell everybody yuh name.
Gwaan truuu me fren,

An nuh bada switch.
Me deh a de end a wait fi yuh get rich...

MISSING YOU (MOM)

As I pause and reminisce,
I know how much we'll miss
A beauty so pure and true,
Oh mommy what will we do?
I've gotten so used to seeing that beautiful smile,
And though I'm no longer a child,
Those times you'd wipe my tears
And dispel horrid fears.
We can't believe you're gone away,
We hope to see you soon someday.
You meant the world to me and always will.
Lord take this pain but can you this emptiness fill?
You are missed so much,
So many lives you've touched.
Your family and friends all miss you so,
Oh we hate to see you go..
But we find joy in knowing someday,
If we never go astray,
We'll be greeted with your loving smile
And it'll be worth our while.
We shall walk upon the sea of glass,
Never an unhappy moment pass.
For we'll be by Jesus' side
Feeling no more pain
Being no longer tried.
Until we see you then,
Thanks for being a friend.
You definitely will be truly missed,
Here's a hug and a kiss.
Here's also saying, sleep tight to you
Mommy, daughter, grandma, aunty, friend….
We'll be missing you.

NO MORE LIES

With theatrical encore, your pretence of care is flaunted.
Two sides of the same coin as you smile with the sunrise and seek my demise with its setting.
You care, only for you.
My tears appear to be a trophy to the gods, an apparel worthy of your boasts
And with your chest held high a gladiator of my brokenness
You say you care, yet as I'm punished by life itself your seat is first class, front row in the VIP section.
In the quick sand of time I am no victor, yet you hold the hands of the clock as you smile and say," it's all good ",
With no care for the sinking....
No more lies.
Care to the wind as another soul is demolished.
No one even noticing the rose without its colour, faded into nothingness.
The sunset without the sun, overshadowed by darkness.
The hymn without a refrain as a voice is lost, the melody stolen, drowned in sorrows.
Your eyes are open but you choose not to see,
No more lies.
So I'm swallowed up again and again,
Now I'm no more.
Only a vague memory and could have beens, I'm just a shell without its host,
Barren and empty just waiting for that last exhale......so like the serpents tongue,
With smooth lies you tell the mass, I stand within inches of my being and declare…No more lies!!

MY PROMISE TO YOU

I promise to make you mine.
I need you now more than ever.
Please be mine till the end
Of time.
I saw me in your eyes, I know this is forever.
I know you are scared
And so am I.
I started falling when I knew you cared.
I no longer want to die.
I just need you to know
I'll always have your back.
My love for you can only grow,
It'll always be on track.
"A friend in need is a friend in deed."
I've always heard people say
And this will always be my creed,
Comes whatever may.

MY LONELY HEART

There she was so misunderstood
And alone,
Beauty uncircumcised from her heart
To her bone.
She had a deep longing
For a gem as rare as she.
I was swept away
And fell in love with me.
I held her hands at nights
When her tears wouldn't let her be.
Yes, it's true, she had no one else but me.
Her nature is kind as it is grand,
So many a time I had to take her hands.
Oh how she loves to smile,
It lights up the darkest room.
No brighter light is there,
No, not even the moon.
She loves to sing and
Dance salsa
And there's always more to learn
Here and thereafter.
She writes poetry
And plays the guitar,
She longs to love
She hates the war.
Must keep her by my side
This time forth
And forever more.
Always here, protecting
Her hearts door.

NOTHING BUT ME

I see the starry skies,
The moonlight night,
The sweet palm trees,
There is nothing but me.
The colours of romance
Gives light to my path,
My depression dancing on oblivions wrath.
Tortoise feeling building up at gauge,
My emotions soon war will wage.
I get on my legs,
I stand on my feet,
I look around, but no one I see.
There’s still nothing but me.
Tis at dark and the lonely place,
When you're standing face to face with despair, desolation,
It is a thing that destroys an entire nation.
I cry in anguish, you can't understand my language.
For no sorrow you know your life is an easy flow.
So I fall to my knees
When no one I see,
Still, there's nothing but me.
I climb the thorns in life's rose bed
Though the smell is sweet, if you fall you're dead.
On eagles wings I soar,
But the darkness grows more and more.
I’m swept away, can't work can't play.
The night darkens my path and oh with such cruel wrath!
Oh light? Light? A flicker even,
Shine down on a poor fool a grieving.
Something reached down.
Something touched me,
I looked around, but no one I see.
Still, there's nothing but me.

THE NARCISSIST

You took away the flavour of my soul.
You made it your one single goal.
My dreams trampled on, I no longer glowed.
Half the truth has never been told.
Never understood a bone in me.
Imprisoned my heart, no trace of glee.
Forgotten dreams and cinematic nightmares,
A lifetime of regrets and unrealized cares.
Eons in time and silence symphony,
You never even thought to fight for me.
Like moments in time, from your heart I did fade,
In ponds of my tears, you did wade.

SO SAD

Thought you had it all,
Saw you walking tall.
Got paid for a work you did not do
So to me, there was no value.
I watched and saw you so glad,
Too bad I'll make you sad.
Sang so many sad songs,
So many times you did me wrongs.
Put up with failure and mistakes,
Many disappointments and heartbreaks.
I know I'll miss you so bad,
Sometimes life is so sad.
Now an anchor you try to fit,
I've made up my mind to do it.
Took zircon for glass
How long could it last?
Gave you all I had,
Too bad it's oh so sad.

SO DEEP

Like a cool breeze near the sun scorched
Sand,
He reached down and touched
My hand.
My spirit welcomed the familiar
Yearning of his aching heart,
Seemingly lost and torn apart.
He understood me like none
Other could,
I, in my newly awakened state felt
That I would,
Rise to all life is meant to be.
No one can do it, only me.
He saw through me as plain as day,
He made the sun come out to play.
I hope our spirits will dance in the wind,
Cause to be lonely,
Must be a sin.
Yes, it must be so sublime,
As our hearts dance till the end of time.
I think I get him the way he gets me,
Oh, if it's only our destiny.

SO BEAUTIFUL

Each day that passes only confirms how I feel.
You came into my life,
You made me heal.
Only tears of joy flow from a place I've never been
And in my darkest night
Your light never dimmed.
Such an aura you possess,
You are built with such finesse.
You kissed me and took my breath away,
You make me want to stay, forever and a day.
I love the way you love me,
And I love to love you too.
To lose you would be quandary…
My skies would no longer be blue.
Hold me in your arms, please never let me go.
Like fireworks,
Let your feelings show.

TAKE IT

My heart loves you,
So does my soul.
I desire to lay beside you,
So priceless like gold.
Your lips so crimson and pure,
They were the keys to my heart's door.
Let’s just take it,
You know we can't fake it.
One single dance,
Epic moment of sweet romance.
Take my heart, but never break it.
I’m yours from the start, so we can't fake it.
If you feel you’ve won what you deserved,
Why don’t you take it?
A love like this with no reserve,
No one can ever fake it.

SOMEWHERE IN MY HEART

Inside my soul, there's no music to a song.
Inside my soul, there's no need to belong.
Somewhere in my heart of hearts, I'm tired of the hurt.
In those lonely corners inside of me,
Emptiness does lurk.
I'm bruised and battered,
I'm torn to shreds.
All other feelings doesn't matter,
I feel as if I'm dead.
No star in sight, no sun nor moon.
No reason for a smile,
No rain in the month of June.
For some stability, for a little joy,
A thousand miles, my feet to employ.
With the rising sun, etched a little smile
As insurmountable trials upon me,
Do pile.
As thin as paper, as barren as land,
Can thou my journey understand?
So I die daily from a thousand hurts.
It seems death with me now flirts.
Maybe I'll meet my maker,
Or the undertaker.
So yes,
I'm dead, I died today,
If only to seal my hurt.
I'm dead again from tears I've cried,
Now place me under the earth.

THAT NIGHT

After that romantic interlude, I found myself
In the afterglow.
Memories of you breathing down my neck,
Our blood boiled with passion.
Oh how I yearn to feel you inside me!
Every inch of my being, desires to be one with you.
Oh how your body beckons to me.
Your smile, like waves in the ocean.
Your eyes like the early sunset and mmmm,
The way our tongues entwine
And move to the music of our hearts as they save each other...
Oh can this be real?
"Is this really happening? "I ask myself.
In the still of the moment, I find myself wanting,
Wanting to be one with you.
Pierce me, deeply!
Feel the heat of my flesh as it engulfs your love muscle,
Aaaaaah it's just as good as I hoped it would be,
As our bodies erupt and explode in ecstasy.

THAT IS LIFE

Though the sky is dark it may not rain,
For the sky has to get dark,
Another day to gain.
Though the sky is bright,
You may not see the light,
For they are hidden in life's
Dark clouds
Out of sight.
When our burdens get heavy
And we can't go on,
Look over your shoulder
Your ounce, to his ton.
For every table that's set,
There is always people to eat.
Some may even get upset,
Of the quandary that lay at their feet.
If we feed one today,
Ten may die tomorrow.
At least for that one,
There's one less sorrow.
There is no ending to anything that starts,
For it begins right here in our hearts.
Which when we die
Will continue to exist,
Our prolific nature cannot resist.

THE PIANO

In life there will be highs and lows,
Flats and sharps.
Whites, only heavenly glows...
Blacks, you'll never hear harps.
There is never one without the other,
If even for a time.
Life is never without a care or bother,
Never always sublime.
Yet,
When the two are played together
What sweet harmony it brings.
Good or bad life is a treasure.
Blacks or whites, beautiful things.
The piano makes sweet music on this journey called life.
Only to be treasured and played with no need for strife.
Play on sweet piano, encore.
Lifting my voice to life, on eagles wings
I'll soar.

THE STRANGER

As our too brief a meeting comes to an end of fast forwardness,
So much you said without a word's utterance, I heard you.
Silent symphony told me all that escaped those beautiful browns with depths like the abyss of the oceans' floors, so beautifully silent and mysterious.
As you return from the land where everything is possible, in visions of the Night, your thoughts escaped to touch her face. That smile and the voice of that stranger you met, slapping the subconscious with violent reckoning of sorts.
With eonic distance they both stare in the same heaven and wonder about that brief meeting so fascinating
An exchange of aura to ignite the senses and soothe the mind.
He hides behind those beautiful browns,
That shouts sentiments unbridled
Saying things that would make an angel blush.
I see you, I feel you...
The stranger.

MY WISH

Some flowers are called Roses,
Some are called Forget Me Nots.
Let the sweet smell of life curl up our noses,
Evading all evil Plots.
Whatever life may bring you,
This one thing is true.
Hope you'll have a beautiful day,
Bringing only the best things your way.

WHEN I SMILE

When I smile, do you believe me?
What exactly do you see?
Do you believe my eyes when they smile at you?
Not everything you see, is true.
Clandestine like cares hidden deep within,
On pivots of time few battles to win.
This smile holds me hostage to all I know,
Laconic replies concealing my woe.
A mirage of sorts to fool the crowd,
A silence so deep a whisper so loud.
A whirlwind of cares, arresting my brain,
An eruption of sorrows which cannot be tamed.
I smile masking within the murky depths of the deep,
That no one can within my soul peep.
When I smile the story is more than you'll see,
When I smile my heart, not necessarily filled without glee.
Yet on the flip side of every coin,
Duplicity will often join.
When I smile, I'll light up a room.
Really, it came from the light of the moon.
Yet my feelings will often beguile,
This I often do, when I smile.

THE VICTIM

You misunderstood my longing,
You ignored my pain.
Didn't even know the gem that was hanging
Before your face,
Like the pouring rain.
Took me for granted, I fell so easy.
You took the love I planted,
Without even trying to please me.
I made you my king,
I gave you my all.
You became my everything,
Now you will make me feel small.
My heart has never glowed the way it glowed for you,
For a season I thought you felt the same way too.
Trying to decide,
To do what must be done.
It's taking quite some time,
My heart and my mind aren't
United in the same song.
My mind tells me to leave
but my heart says" keep hanging on"
I hate the way I love you,
Oh I wish that I could cease.
The way my heart yearns, it's true,
You're every wish to please.
If you would value me and make me your queen,
I'd show you colours of love
Like you've never seen.
I'd make you so happy I swear,
I'll never make you blue.
I'd make it so you'd never forget me,
We'd be one never again two.
With deepest regret and sadness of over a thousand years,
To you my love I say goodbye.

My heart is filled with tears,
It feels as if I’ll die.
I’ve left you for me,
I really hope you'll understand.
It’s my heart's deepest tragedy,
I really wanted you to be my man.

MY ROOM

It’s five am and I woke up with you on my mind.
I’m guessing it was so designed.
It’s not about Lust.
No just,
The way you make me feel,
You have such great appeal.
Has cupid gone lost his mind?
For you aren't really mine.
My heart makes a thousand quakes,
It’s not just a touch.
That's all it takes
For you are my only crush.
Thoughts of you   rock my world,
Will I ever be your girl?
Pitter patter, pitter patter,
Goes my heart around you.
You are my paper
And I'm your Glue.
You smile and light the pathway to my heart,
You illuminate it quietly, with only a spark.
This house is filled with cold walls and the musty Rooms.
Loud shrieks and screams of doom.
You are my hero,
That makes them zero.
There’s now no pain or impending doom,
Simply because you stepped into my room.

NO WAY OUT

The more things change, the more they stay the same.
When things seem to get better,
They change the name of the Game.
Pulling the ground from under my feet,
Where tragedies in every form meet.
Seems when one thing is fixed, the other gets broken,
As if it needs my heart for a token.
To brag about pain worn like a Curtain,
To complicate and make life uncertain.
In the midst of drowning, I grasped a straw.
While cruel serpents at my clutch did gnaw.
Unravelling my firm grip on life,
Just short of cutting with a Knife.
I'm above water, now on the sand.
Yet still, how long shall I stand?
I'm yet unstable for a season,
Until life has a reason
To unleash all the challenges at hand,
Just to see, if still I shall stand.

THAT'S LIFE

Though the sky is dark, it may not Rain,
For the sky has to get dark
Another day to Gain.
Though the sky is bright,
You may not see the light,
For they are hidden in life's
Dark clouds out of Sight.
When our burdens get heavy
And we can't go on,
Look over your shoulder and you will see,
Your ounce to his ton.
For every table that's set,
There is always people to eat.
Some may even get upset
Of the quandary that lay s at their feet.
If we feed one today,
Ten may die tomorrow;
But at least for that one,
There’s one less sorrow.
There is no ending to anything that starts,
For it begins right here in our hearts.
Which when we die
Will continue to exist.
Our prolific nature cannot resist.

RIDE OR DIE ME

Uplift me, gift me
But never ever drift me.
Trust me, hug me
But never ever thug me
I can be ya......must me, trust me
So don't ever dust me.
Kiss me, feel me
Get to know the real Me.
Cloud me, proud me
But never ever shroud me.
I can be your ride or die me,
Never ever lie me,
Fly me, dine me but never ever cry me.
Hold me, boldly
Never ever cold Me.
Bless me, text me
But never ever vex me.
I can be your ride or die me.
Come on baby why don't you try Me.?

YOU CAME

You came, when the sun refused to shine.
You came, turning water into wine.
You came, when my blue clouds turned to grey.
You came, chasing them all away.
You came, when my heart was torn asunder.
You came, with such power and thunder.
You came, and swept me off my feet.
You came, and oh what a treat.
You came, when I thought I could love no more.
You came, and oh what a love so pure.
You came, and I gave you my everything.
You came, and I soared on eagle's wings.
You came, and I'll never forget you.
You came, and I'm so in love with you.
You came, yes you took my breath away.
You came, made me happy forever and a day.
You came and my days will never be the same.
No hurt nor pain,
Only sunshine no rain.
Never be lonely again,
.... Simply because you came.

YOU'RE NOT ALONE

Sometimes I'm sick and tired of being sick and tired.
Don't wanna stand or sit,
Neither water nor fire,
And the important, can't remember it.
Life is a journey and to each his own.
It's always good to have a friend so you won't be alone.
To be by your side now and always,
To be there to lighten your days.
Though we can't take the pain
To be your sunshine, never your rain,
We'll ask God above for mercy and for grace
So finish this race just ask him for help, he'll never turn you away.
To prove it, he's coming for his little
Ones, some sweet day.

PEACE

Like lilies in the blowing wind,
Like cherries on a tree,
I'd like to find eternal peace within,
Or simply to ever at peace be.
As the ocean caresses the sea shore,
I long for a love forevermore.
Come oh peaceful life, come oh happy home.
No more, no more strife, for my heart to moan.
Like sweet music to the lonely ear,
Provision for a lonely heart, is love and care.
I know someday I'll find all that I seek
If I remain persevering and meek.
Oh please peace, just hurry my way
And then forever stay.

THE SUN

The sun hugged the sky this morning
Did you see?
Dancing birds in the sky, they pointed at me
“Look at her!" they all seemed to say,
And I felt a kiss when the breeze
Blew my way.
The trees recited my movements, yes,
My every sway.
I never knew how beautiful the sky
Grew being rolled back as a scroll...
A brand-new day to behold.
A kiss from the morning dew
Oooh, there's so much I never knew.
I’m alive today, I hope forever
And a day,
To feel the embrace of the sun
For my life has only just begun.

WITHOUT YOU

The whispers of silent sorrow slowly becoming louder and louder,
No longer silent. The salt of agony and despair,
There is no joy or happiness here.
For now it's just ugly feelings that are torturous for any willing soul to bear.
Moping and tearfulness are all I know now,
I have lost the ability to smile, to love to exist even.
Each day without you is just agony.
Pain accompanied by confusion.
It’s inevitable though, this path I've trod,
I understand it's a part of the journey.
If some crazy soul could just bear this for me,
Share this with me.
But …..No one is willing to lay down their very existence for me.
For …..To feel this way is to give up existing.
It’s just dwelling.
Dwelling in a world,
Without people…
Without air,
Without the one I love,
Without you.

TRUTH BE TOLD

I miss you so my brother
A love like ours so bold,
Is quite unlike any other.
I miss our walks,
Our talks about life.
With probity of heart,
This distance cuts like a knife.
A love like ours so perpetual and true
And for a brother no one else will do.
I love you with a love that spans a
Thousand years.
I want to be there always to dry
Your tears.
With a ponderous heart, I wish you well my brother.
Cause a love like ours,
There's simply no other
I love you.

LIFE

Each person you meet is like that unread book, untraversed pages to
Ignite the imaginings.
Some of these pages from horror scenes forbidden. Others from beauty and the beast,
And yet others... From out of this world like the sci fi of life.
Monotony makes for poor reading as poor mortar, the clay.
Yet, when life gives us this rare diamond, most times uncut,
We see only a clear glass. Much to our demise.
Accept the minute gifts of life. Accept the thorns that come with the roses.
Life in prolificity of our inner wants and desires.
Treasuring each friend like no other.
Giving your love at no expense to your soul.
Touching every heart with warmth and compassion.
Living life to its fullest,
Giving of all that's unique only to you.

WHAT IF

What if I went away?
Would you miss the words I used to say?
What if you could turn back the hands of time?
Would you wish I'd make you mine all mine?
What if you woke and I was only a dream?
Would you sigh or maybe scream?
What if I could turn your water into wine?
Would you think I was so divine?
What if I said I love you?
Would you say you love me too?
What if I kissed you and took your breath away?
Would it always be that way?
What if we were free?
Would you ever marry me?
What if I gave you my all?
Would you in turn make me stand tall?
What if this poem was dedicated to you?
What would u say, to me too?

THE TREE

With wanton disregard, he did it.
Made his appearance, made you love him,
Then he just up and quit.
What have I done wrong?
I sung for so long.
This coming I could not see,
Then I remembered about the tree.
The tree has leaves, that aren't meant to stay.
As time progresses, they fall away.
With no care, very little reason at all,
Some people leave causing others to fall.
Then there is the stem that is attached to the leaves.
A little tighter these people seem to Cleave.
Yet at the sign of any trouble
They'll leave you on the Double.
So as the wind blows the leaves fall to the ground,
Not even making a sound.
Then branches that hold the stem,
Many won't ever forget them.
They will stay,
Sometimes forever and a Day.
Until that major disaster,
No one can run any faster.
Sometimes… they are chopped off by the hands of time.
You feeling a victim of the crime.
So the hurricane has left with them.
Those people you thought were friends.
Now the root, holds all this these together.
They are those who stay forever.
No small wind, disaster nor time,
Will these roots ever leave you behind?
They'll be there, when others have split,
Always holding the tree, won't ever quit.
These are the friends to treasure and hold dear.

There for you, through sorrow or fear
So hurricanes come and go but the roots of the trees often remain.
Ready to start over again and again.

SECTION TWO: LOVE

In different times and places in our lives, we fall in love. Sometimes it's that awesome man that takes our breath away. There are times when it's our children and yet another time when we come into our own and learn to self-love and appreciate....me.

MY DARLING DAUGHTER

To never miss is to never have loved,
And I really love you.
To never love is to never exist, you make my dreams
Come through.
I am nothing without you.
Being away from you has simply
Made me blue.
I miss the way you smile and the way you call my name,
As small as you are, you are there for me
Whenever I'm in pain.
I'm simply crazy about you my darling daughter.
Tears have stained the place where there once was laughter.
I long to hear your voice,
Feel your arms about my neck,
Being without you my life's a total wreck.
I count the days, the hours and the minutes
Till we're together again,
And never forget you're not only my daughter,
You're also my best friend.

DADDY (A FATHER'S DAY WISH)

Some things weren't meant to be.
Bad things happen to you, to me.
We can never tell what might have been.
We can never tell why a bright light should go dim.
I know she'd really be loving you,
There'd be no separating the two.
You'd be the star in her darkest sky...
Always wiping her tears, kissing each eye.
If she was here, I know what she'd want to say.
She'd say, "Daddy, my daddy, Happy Father's Day."

FOREVER

Sweetheart I'm gonna love you with all my length of days,
And if you could see my love for you, you'd truly be amazed.
I'll cherish every moment of you and me together,
And we'll share mountains of joy forever and ever!
There's this special way you make me feel,
And nothing's ever felt so real.
From the first time I saw your lovely face
And felt your warm embrace,
I've needed to belong to you.
Now it's forever true.
We've been through so much together,
And you never let me go.
This love of ours is forever!
And now the whole world will know.
So now, I give my heart to you,
To forever love and be true.
I'll love you in good times and bad,
Cause darling you're all I had.
Till death do us part,
And even then you're forever in my heart.
So sweetheart here is my sincere vow to you,
Lover, spouse and friend
Forever I do forever…
Forever I do.

ASHANTI

I remember your face on that beautiful day.
Seeing you made my heart race
As you in my arms lay.
So pretty, so cute,
Just like I thought you would be.
To my heart you found the route from now to eternity.
I loved you then,
And even more now.
I hope our friendship never ends,
And to you I make this vow.
I'll always be by your side
As long as I shall live.
As long as there is breath in me,
To you my heart I give.
Mommy loves you.

ENDLESSLY

Thinking of you is all I really do
And no matter where I go, baby you're always on my mind.
I miss you endlessly.
You've become a much to me as the very air I breathe.
My arms knew no longing until I met you.
Be still my heart for your pounding wakes me from my dreams.
Dreams of me holding you, wanting you endlessly.
Tell me, are you ready for love?
Love in its purest and truest form...me?
Give me the chance to make you happy let me love you endlessly.
I am your beacon of light, to let your heart tremble with excitement.
To make your lips curl at the sides in pleasure.
Though tears may fall, they'll be tears of joy.
I'll make you happy endlessly.
Bring out the best in me, let me love you endlessly.
If you make me laugh I'll cherish you endlessly.

DAYDREAM

I lie awake with thoughts of you.
You are my cloud's silver lining,
To you I'll ever be true.
You came along like the prince for Cinderella
And as the story ends, you're forever my fella.
You make me laugh.
You make me smile.
So for you I'd walk a thousand miles.
You treat me the way I know I deserve.
You give me your everything,
With very little in reserve.
You are so shy and sweet, yet I know you are deeper.
Let me into your life, I'll make everything sweeter.
You've given to me what I once had, but lost.
You sought to give it back to me at all cost.
Let's be true to each other, let's be the best of friends.
Let's deal with whatever comes our way,
No matter how the story ends.

MY VALENTINE?

I shy away at the mention of your name.
Expressions, I hide when your eyes at me aim.
If I could just let you know,
That I truly love you so.
I'm ready to live again,
I feel I'd take the risk.
Won't you just come…?
Please from me this lonely heart whisk?
Do I dare confront you and say….
You're the love of my life?
Do I dare tell you I'd say yes, I'd gladly be your wife?
It's the season for lovers at least for today please be mine.
With every beat of my lonely heart,
Won't you be my valentine?

YOU

Lying here with you beside me
I feel something inside,
Glad I have you here to guide me
My lover and my pride.
When my journey here has ended,
My truth will be my progeny.
My broken heart which has ended,
Is no longer quandary.
Helping to renew my esteem
And gave me back my confidence.
A gaze from your eyes so pristine
A belief in self to commence.
Thanks for being you,
Please don't ever change.
Helping to make my dreams come through,
My life to rearrange.

THOUGHTS OF YOU

My heart dances to the rhythm of your breath against my cheek,
My thoughts of you making me weak.
Cascades of feelings rushing down my spine,
Memories of you so sublime.
Touch my face
So gentle and sweet.
As I, like butter,
Melt to your feet
It's raining now and
My thoughts of you
Convey your fingers
On the touch of my skin,
As I smile and I take you in.
I like the music
We dance to now,
Familiar rhythm as
We turn and take a bow.
Rest your lips on my face
And feel this warm embrace,
As I close my eyes and
Dance to the rhythm of your song.

LOVE 2

Love, like life, is so uncertain, so give it your all
Before the final curtain.
No one knows what tomorrow may bring,
So love life, it's your everything.
Love every day, and love every second of loving.
Hold her, squeeze her, no push
No shoving.
Smile for it's healthy and it goes a far way.
Smiling is a part of loving, it can give your heart away.
Take hold of love don't let it pass you by,
Or you'll just be sitting around,
Rivers of tears go by as you cry
Because love has come, and it slipped away.
Now you're sad with each passing day.
With sayings of "if only I knew, it's a chance I would take
Cause now I'm loveless,
I've decided my fate."

MY LOVE

Come my love, let me take your coat.
Sit and the rest your weary feet. Here let me take off your shoes,
Aaah... isn't that better?
Come my love, give me your hair.
Let me wash away the sweat that has so stained.
Lean back, don’t be tense …
Relax, let me caress your chest,
Your love muscles,
Your entire… you.
Come my love,
Step into this towel
While I dry your wet body.
Yes, lay
On this bed while I dry every unnecessary stream.
Let me oil your sensuously warm body
That continues to beckon to me.
Come my love for I fear I can't resist.
That’s it!
Kiss me right here...
Right there….
Wait, wait, and let me dim the lights,
Honey please be gentle.
Come my love,
Let’s make love.
Let’s make…. love

TALLY

I saw a little girl this morning,
She was no more than two.
I smiled as I remembered you.
Tears filled my eyes as I remembered our love.
It was something special, sent from above.
Wish I could say I love you now more than ever before.
But the truth is you opened my heart's door,
The minute I saw your lovely face
And you, I did embrace.
I am proud of who you turned out to be.
Someone who adores your family.
I’ve made mistakes, no I’m not perfect
As I sit and yet reflect.
Yet, I must have done something right,
You turned out so beautiful and bright.
With all my heart, I love you so
And I just want the whole world to know,
In the midst of tears and laughter
I couldn't ask for a better daughter.

SUMMER LOVE

Your love like summer so warm and bold.
A love to cherish to have and to hold.
With smile like sunshine a lion to tame …
Rain or shine I'll still feel the same.
The colours of me only you will see,
Like torrents of rain,
My feelings to tame.
The rays I feel upon my face,
I feel in the wind your warm embrace.
A kiss on my neck like the morning dew.
In moments of time my love only grew.
So of all the seasons that's sent from above,
There’s no other like a summer love.

THE CRUSH

So smitten you are by me,
I see more than you think.
You make me the vine of your tree,
I see the stares without a blink.
Testosterone working it's magic
In you,
I'm your everything.
Grey skies are always blue,
Right now, you can hear angels sing.
Such manliness possess you,
Oh what care and defence.
Seems as though you will always be true,
Your feelings are no pretence.
You are so young,
Don't quite understand valleys and hills.
I can't be the lyrics in your song,
No not the one who gives you chills.
Maybe if time wasn't a foe,
A light to your candle I'd bring.
Such a far way we could go,
I'd make you my everything.
Just keep being you,
Don't ever change.
People like you are way too few,
So totally out of range.
One day she'll come knocking on your door,
When you least expect.
For your love she'll be the cure,
She'll have your utmost respect.
You'll love her so and she'll love you.
No greater love will there be,
Her love to you will be so true and
I? Only be a memory.

LOVE

Love is a gift that can't be taken away.
It always stays with me each passing day.
Love can't be bought, neither can it be sold.
Yet love is more precious than silver or gold.
Love is for everyone,
It's for you it's for me.
Love is free,
It was placed on a tree.
It was freely given without regret.
Love was there for me,
Even though we never met.
Love is here to stay,
To be with us through and through.
Love is forever. It's for me, it's for you.

LOVE POETRY

Roses are everything we want them to be.
Red, sweet smelling and beautiful you see.
Violets are forever, gorgeously blue.
Whoever gives you one of these,
Will forever be true.
Put them together they make a wonderful gift.
Given to your soul mate, will surely their spirits lift.
Be careful of this gift you've made.
For if you're not true, these flours will surely fade.
So be true to whomever it may be,
Always filling their hearts with glee.
As roses are red and violets are blue,
To your lover, always be true.

I LOVE YOU

You've captured my heart with your you.
You fall in a place where only a few,
I chose to invite in my space,
Forgetting the chase.
Your inner you is so deep,
Way so sweet.
You kiss my blues away,
Groove and sway,
Groove and sway.
I close my eyes I feel you
Reach you, touch you.
Your hands on my soul,
Stealing all that's making me whole.
As if it's not forever, here when ever and a day.
In your arms I am clay.
As I breathe you in,
Something deep within.
I'm giving you me
And I want your ...you.
Come and bask with me
Let our love break through
Boundaries that were set,
Though we never met.
I just need your inner you.
Need you to be my boo,
I'm so in love with you.
My love I swear it's true,
Nobody for me but you.
I love you.

IF ONLY

If only you knew
All the things I would do.
If only to be with you,
To show my love is true.
Oh, I'm empty without you,
My skies are no longer blue.
My love for you is true
And for you there's nothing I wouldn't do.
If only I could make you smile,
For even a while.
As happy as a child,
In his mother's arms, so
Yet quite agile.
It'll be worth my while
To walk me down the aisle.
So as I go,
I want you to know,
I love you so.
Don't let me go.
Our love can only grow,
Let our love flow.
It would be so awesome,
If only you'd know.

EXHALE

You reached down, touched a place inside of me.
A place not easily reached.
Made all of my sadness flee,
Against this kind most preachers have preached.
Your kiss was sudden, but came, in the nick of time.
Then when you bit my breasts, I knew you had to be mine.
You then laid on top of me,
How u spread my legs
And placed yourself inside so carefully,
I felt the need to beg.
I sighed because you took my breath away,
Such passion …….I felt so much need.
To rock to your world with every sway,
My every desire to feed.
Oh from behind you entered with utter care and devotion.
You rocked my world with every move,
The only boat in the ocean.
The sounds you make, you cannot fake,
I knew I was blowing your mind.
I held you tight, it was so right
You were mine at the drop of a dime.

DESIRE

I need to soar with you more and more,
Let's fly away together.
I want you, that's for sure,
Have each other's back forever.
These feelings I can't ignore,
My desire for you is ever so great.
Please stay with me I do implore,
I feel my love just can't wait…
To be with you all the days of my life,
I hope someday to be your wife.

ETERNALLY

Some friendships are forged of memories, some quite clear.
Some forged of experiences, that we hold dear.
Others forged, of what's thought was meant to be,
Others forged of gold eternally.
Whatever the reason, it should be forever.
Nothing the test of time should break, not ever.
Something the moon and stars envy,
It's rare.
Filled with love in the absence of fear.
May this friendship we share though brief it may be,
Be like the love that was placed on a tree.
Let it be envied by all who now see,
How special a friend you are to me.

COLORS OF ME

What are the colours of a rainbow?
Colours …. Emotions and feelings of love ecstasy,
That shine from without to within.
Rainbows of never- ending colors, the way you make me feel.
Red….The bold never ending gushes of passion.
Blue ….. The calm tingle of quietness.
Green …. Fresh mountains of feelings climbing higher and higher,
Yellow … The radiance of my inner being that I give to you my love.
Black …..The despair and desolation of thoughts of leaving you or you leaving me.
Purple ….the feeling, the truth that no queen could be in finer colours than this royalty, me.
This pedestal from which I should never step down.
This dream oh shall I awake?
Shall all I see from today be only shades of black and white?
Will I ever be happy again?
I want to be quenched by the beauty that lies deep within you.
To be engulfed by erotic passions.
We ignite, yet never burn away.
We explode, yet we never die.
I wish I could give you this part of me
That's forbidden,
That's put away, but not lost.
You didn't get, it but it really belongs to you.
If you stop looking you'll find it.
This rainbow is free God gives it to everyone that will partake of it.
No one else can have this part of me I give to you,
The colours of love…
I love you.

CONFUSION OF LOVE

Anger is my disposition,
Fury my friend.
Jealousy my companion,
Oh when will it end?
For a moment of ice watery calm
Yes quickly,
Before I do harm.
I am cool yet
Heated,
Often repeated.
Sorrowful, yet happy,
Feeling so crappy.
This state of strange confusion is
Quandary to my soul.
Feels like utter fusion,
Yet none can make me whole.
I am yet to decipher,
My here ever after.
I long to have more knowledge,
Cause for love there is no college.

A MOTHER'S LOVE

A Mother's love, oh what a perfect gift!
Only God's love is greater than this.
A mother's love extends beyond the reaches of the universe.
Moves every mountain and breaks every curse.
She loves relentlessly those children she bore,
She'll love them always and forever more.
A mother's love is arduous, vibrant and true.
She gives of her all when there's nothing left to do.
A mother's love is just what it was meant to be,
And it will remain that way throughout eternity.
God saw every babe and said, "I'll give you the best gift ever made.
I'll give you a mother who'll love you like none other,
For nothing, you…she would ever trade."

A PRAYER OF HOPE

Dear lord when the trials of life shall take me over,
When my ship of hope has sank.
When my heart's in pieces on the floor,
And there's no fuel left in my tank.
Always be there with outstretched arms to rescue and resuscitate,
Even when others say it's way too late.
When my last breath is soon sucked from me
And oh my body broken,
Abbreviate my life with hope of thee,
Cause life itself is a token.
So with praises high and voices raised,
To you oh God I give my praise .amen.

THAT MAN

There he was in the room, looking so hot,
His legs going on forever to that gorgeous spot.
Thighs like forest trees muscular and grand,
As I" accidentally" passed and rubbed his hand.
So soft and smooth like the creeper in wine,
Oh I wanted to make him mine all mine.
When he flashed that smile,
Those pearly white teeth, I felt
The earth move beneath my feet.
I wasn't having it couldn't lose my cool,
You know my mama never raised no fool.
His masculine scent going up my nose,
As I in that single moment froze.
He was perfect like no other man could,
He stood there, looking good.
I watched his beard, it caressed his face.
His hair neatly cut, nothing out of place.
I held my chest to hyperventilate.
Couldn't let this one go out the gate.
The room light flirted with the tone of his skin.
He walked to my chair something moved within,
“Hello", he said, in that Barry White voice,
“Mam, I’m afraid I had no choice,
Had to come over before anyone else could,
I had to tell you, you are looking good,
I am going over to the bar to sip some wine,
Having your company would be so divine"
I pinched myself although he could not see.
This hunk of a man was talking to me.
I smiled in agreement and held his arm,
His muscles so thick, his body so warm.
We had a few drinks a dance or two,
To Manhattans, Shylights, rhythm and blues.
Exchanged numbers, he walked me to my car.

He knew I wasn't going too far.
A slight kiss on my cheek, he said, “goodbye.”
Oh I was really into this guy!
He waved goodbye standing under the moon,
The sweetest guy standing in the room.

VALENTINE (LYRICS)

Roses are red, Violets are blue
I wrote this valentine poem just for you.
Trees are green while the earth is round,
Sweetheart, I promise I'll always be around.
Water has no colour and air you can't see,
Baby I'm glad you're lying next to me.
The sun is hot while snow is cold,
With you my dear I want to grow old.
Mountains are high and valleys are low,
My love for you will only grow and grow.
The rainbow has many colours,
And so do many flowers,
I could keep writing this poem for hours and...Hours.

TALENA

There you were so tiny and brave,
And before our eyes ever met,
Oh your love I did crave.
Always so bright,
You light up any room.
You brightened up my day,
From you entered my womb.
So bright you are
Beyond your years
You are my shining star,
Dispelling all my fears.
Had our share of ups and downs,
Many times we wore our frowns.
But I determined to never give up
On you
So we'd always be one,
Even though we are two.
I know I make mistakes as parents
Often do,
But it's all because, my child
I so love you.
I didn't get the manual of parenting,
If ever one was made
And though at times you vented
A trade, I never made.
Talena you are special, you mean the world to me
And I'll feel this way from now till eternity.
Mommy loves you.

LOVE ME SOME

I love me some love, life
Filled with toppings of sunshine and rays of hugs.
I love me some me,
Radiant, a vibrant beauty, no need for thugs.
I love me some you,
Volcanic flares, sparks of a forest fire.
I love me some life, keyholes void of locks, higher heights to aspire.
I love me some time, excavating hidden treasures, the beauty in you.
I love me some breakups,
Then only the best make ups will do.
I love me some isolation,
Locked away serving my sentence in your arms.
I love me some hard labour, beads of sweat bursting,
As I'm melted by your charms.
I love me some words,
To express my prolific desires.
I love some lyrics,
To ignite your fires.
I love me this poem,
A masterpiece in the making.
I love me that man,
Worthy enough for the undertaking.

NINA

Sweet dew upon a weary soul,
Fresh water anew.
Higher than the heavens above,
For there's none other like you.
Shouldering mountains of love,
Echoing rivers like dove,
Shout to you sweet songs of forever.
My Nina I'll leave you never.
Everything I am, I owe to you
As in seasons of forever,
Our love only grew.
I am yours, and you are mine,
Our love will always last till the end of time.
Out of my body you came,
Your grandma gave you your name.
You filled our lives with love
And laughter,
Yes it was you,
My darling daughter.

I'M HERE

As I close my eyes
I think of you,
My only desire is to make your dreams come through.
As I sit and ponder,
How much you are a wonder.
With such a sweet and honest presence,
Filled with only benevolence.
I don't know what is hurting you so
But my friend, I only want you to know.
That
At a drop of a dime,
On me, you can call anytime.
I'll never judge, no it's not my place.
I'll never hurt you,
Your heart I will embrace.
Let me be the light that shines within,
And from your heart, my light won't go dim.
Please let me in your heart,
Let's make a brand new start.
No, we'll never part
My love has no dart...
I'm here for you from the start.

LOVE ME SOME

I love me some love, life
Filled with toppings of sunshine and rays of hugs
I love me some me,
Radiant, a vibrant beauty, no need for thugs
I love me some you,
Volcanic flares, sparks of a forest fire
I love me some life,
Keyholes void of locks, higher heights to aspire.
I love me some time, excavating hidden treasures... The beauty in you.
I love me some breakups,
Then only the best make ups will do.
I love me some isolation,
Locked away serving my sentence in your arms.
I love me some hard labour,
Beads of sweat bursting as I'm melted by your charms.
I love me some words,
To express my prolific desires.
I love some lyrics,
To ignite your fires.
I love me this poem,
A masterpiece in the making.
I love me that man,
Worthy enough for the undertaking.
.

SECTION THREE: BELIEVE...

This is feeding our inner selves with the power of victory and.... love... Caressing our egos and manipulating our inner selves to participate in our own evolution.

I PROMISE

You fill me up as I draw you into my heart.
Now we're off to a brand new start.
I promise to never leave,
To have, to hold and to cleave.
I'll make you my shining star
Cause baby that's what you are.
Call on me when you need a friend
Cause I'll be with you till the very end.
I promise to never make you sad or even blue,
Cause baby you know my love is true.
Please make me yours,
As on ocean's floors,
No deeper depths concerning love.
Only something sent from.

ASPIRATIONS

I want to be better.
No, not better than you but better than the me I was yesterday.
I want to evolve to a higher moment in time,
To that place inside of me…
Where greatness hides.
That higher self that awaits my arrival.
Success smiles with me on the horizon,
I feel the cool morning breeze as it echoes sentiments of congrats
And standing ovations.
Encore for my methodic aspirations as I desire only greatness.
As I taste victory, and lend my hand to happiness, I say goodbye to doubts, Procrastination and lovelessness, only to replace it with the crown of the Queen herself. Bestowed in my honour...
My better self now awaits my arrival,
As I anticipate what is to be.
A once in a lifetime taste of the future...
And I look beautiful in it.

CAN'T HURT ME

You can't determine my worth.
Cruel words, starting the birth
Of a true genius that lies within,
Seeking all my glory to dim.
Those words you say to seal my hurt,
Seeks only to unearth
My value that's quite intrinsic.
Listen, I beg to the music.
Of a genius born of pain,
Even though on my parade you tried to rain.
Yet, it was only for a season,
Cause you won't be the reason.
Your opinion has no weight,
You're not the keeper of the gate.
To glory to which my feet now trod the path,
A strong hold on victory with utmost wrath.
You can't hurt me, not any more.
I now all my senses implore.
Stand, in the strength of the lioness in me,
Claiming only victory.

I AM ME

I am the only me, the only me you'll ever see.
I am me affirmed, unique and grand.
I am me, please understand. I am me whether you like it or not
And being me doesn't take a lot.
I am me, won't try to change the colour of my skin,
I am me from somewhere deep within.
I am me, yes there's only one of me,
And that's the world's greatest tragedy.
I am me and I'm quite emotive.
I'll hold no secrets, you'll know my motive.
I am me, I'm INFJ.
I am me, wouldn't have it any other way.
I am me, I believe I can fly.
There's no limit, only the sky.
I am me, even when people say bad things.
I am me, only water off my wings.
I am me, my mistakes won't my value change,
So you my thoughts can't rearrange.
I am me stated quite explicitly.
I am me…
I am me.

LEVEL UP

Who says I need a man to be complete?
A lie from the pit of hell!
I won't for anyone's love compete.
I am worth more than you can tell.
You seh me ago dead alone
That’s only what you think.
You only, made my heart moan,
Ready fi push me ova de brink.
Too long have I settled for less than I’m worth,
Too many a compromise,
Narcissistic man of such girth.
Your words were filled with such lies.
Too long have I waited on a love,
That is deserving of me.
Me naa go fight nor push and shove.
I’ll be the best only for me.
Coming into my life, you'd only be wasting your time.
Naaah sekkle fi less dan me worth.
I’m here for me at a drop of a dime.
No one again will my heart hurt.
The boundaries I’ve set is quite fervent,
nuhh affi balance pon no one eyed serpent,
To tell me how much I’m loved and needed,
Cause my love for me is completed.

THE QUEEN I AM

The Queen I am,
Won't ask you out.
The queen I am,
Her value will never doubt.
The queen I am,
Refuses to be second guessed.
For she knows, she deserves
Only the best.
The queen I am,
I won't doubt.
The queen I am,
Won't vex or pout.
The queen I am allows u to let her go,
What you reap is what you'll sew.
The queen I am,
Sees things she'd rather not say.
The Queen I am,
Will always pray.
The Queen I am,
Won't settle for less.
She knows she deserves only the best.
Well if a queen in me you
Refuse to see,
I will not plea.
Just let me be,
One day you'll see.
What tragedy,
You let me flee.
I am all I am,
It was God's plan.
My life is always grand
Because I know the Queen
I am.

NEW DAY

A kiss on your forehead,
A rose in your bed.
For the challenge you may meet,
That'll surely crumble at your feet.
I hold your hand for the warmth it brings, as on angel's wings.
You tell me to have a beautiful day at work,
And like coffee, you were my perk.
I'm off to face the challenge that this day may pack,
Cause baby I know you got my back.

HAVE FAITH IN ME

When I feel I've done my best and can't quite manage the rest.....
Just have faith in me.
When I've thrown in the towel and now wear a frown
….have faith in me.
Going to work and juggling school,
Can't be managed by any old fool,
Just have faith in me.
At the end of my time,
It will be so sublime.
I'll look at my achievements,
Without any bereavement.
I'll be a better me, for both me and my family.
All because...
You had faith in me.

I DID IT

So proud I am of me,
Standing taller than any tree.
I did what had to be done,
Yes, it was so much fun.
Though the lanterns light wasn't lit,
I stuck it through, I did it.
I made up my mind to capture me.
Now that's done, I feel so free.
I walked a million miles with just one step.
Sleepless nights I haven't slept.
I stuck it through, I didn't quit.
So proud I am that I did it.
I love me more than words can say,
It gets much more each passing day.
When my world came crumbling down,
I bit my lips and made no sound.
On defeats lap I didn't sit,
So proud I am, that I did it.
Silent tears to wet my bed,
Morticians smiled seemed I was dead.
Resilience has become my suit,
No more defeats to recruit.
My enemies cried, they threw a fit!
So proud I am that I did it.
Now I fly from my cocoon,
To greater heights than of the moon.
I'm off to greater things,
Defeat light water off my wings.
Achieved my goals, I'm now a hit!
So proud I am that I did it!!!

ONE MATCH

The only enemy we have sometimes
Is ourselves.
Taking our dreams, putting on shelves.
Procrastination is the killer of dreams.
Some things are never truly as they seem.
Let your one match, make an explosion!
Giving all of your portion…
To be all you can be,
Becoming a part of history.
So reach for that star,
And go no matter how far.
Indulge in yourself, let the flames burn.
Digging deeper let the heart yearn,
For greatness entrenched in the forever parts.
Where all failure ends and greatness starts.
There is greatness on the inside of you,
Step away and from the outside
Take a view.
Look at all life has to offer you,
And always to yourself be true.
You'll only reach as far as you try to go.
It's important for you to know,
The journey of a thousand miles begin with just one step…
So excavate your inner depth.
Where can I make a great impact?
Igniting the world with just one match.

SECTION FOUR: SOUL FOOD

We forget who we are in the race to achieve and attain the physical. Self, passion, romance is often sacrificed....
Let's partake of the goodness of love and be saved from the famine that too often lead to our own demise.....enjoy!

THE DARKNESS

As wooden frames holding a picture, the darkness hugged my soul.
Silent breezes stealing away any semblance of warmth.
Angry reckonings of one more confusing moment,
Life's bitter sweet tragedies strike again!
And gave no time to prepare as hurricane
On dry land.
Being the creeping prey of life's quick sand.
Will there be a silver moon that glitters upon the waters?
Giving light to the angry shadows so trapped within?
Or is it my destiny to be digested by the darkness, never to return?

IN MY DREAMS

In my dreams,
I remember a dream that happened a lifetime or two.
In my dreams,
I had a fantasy, yet another wish come through.
In my dreams, we fell in love and it lasted an eternity.
In my dreams, there was no one else in the world but you and me.
Some say dreams aren't for real they never will come through.
Others say dreams aren't for people like me and like you.
Yet, I know that in believing in dreams we belong.
It’s like putting sweet music to that colourless song.
I dreamt one day, you'll say
"Excuse me, have we met before"?
And I'll gladly say
“Yes, we met when I opened your heart's door.”

THERE'S SILENCE IN ME

There is a silence in me, it's my inner voice.
It's who I speak to, I have no choice.
I feel I am eons away from home.
Painstakingly, my heart seems to roam.
Why can't you hear the words I say?
Oh Potter where is the clay?
To make within complete
Oh my heart where is the beat?
The words I say just blown away
And forever that's where they'll stay.
Not even given a second thought, as though I count as Naught.
There's more to me than meets the eye, sometimes no tears I cry.
I'm completely dry.
Much silence in me, often misunderstood.
Doesn't mean in me, there is no good.
As high as the mountains and as deep as the sea,
My heart is full of fountains, although there is a silence in me.

THINKING OF YOU

I find myself in a moment of time thinking of you
Wondering if you're ok or feeling blue.
Remembering your scent, the colour of your eyes, I feel a rush.
When you smile, my cheeks get blush.
The feel of your skin when upon my face your lips you place.
When you hug me I take you in, Are you by chance, my secret twin?
The energy that escapes my soul,
Seeking only to make you whole.
I see your love as plain as day,
In your arms I'm a morsel of clay.
It seems against my will I've given you my heart.
You navigated the journey from the very start.
To make me fall in love with you,
Forever making my skies blue

WE THREE

It's been quite a while since we've had a staff meeting just us three.
Yes, I, myself and me.
I see myself from time to time,
She’s not doing too bad these days, she's pretty fine.
I asked myself, “is it all worth it the struggles we endure?”
I also asked me, “will it get better for sure?"
Yet in us three do I trust, I’ll be strong for us I really must.
Me? I'm doing fine.
A little struggle from time to time.
Yet we three, myself I and me,
We have each other's back.
There’s nothing else we lack.
There are times I get upset and would have the need to vent,
Yet I won't trouble myself, for from her troubles she won't relent.
They both sit and have a talk with me
To find the best solution you see.
Inside us all,
Is the need to call...
Upon that one deep inside to defend,
Some other hand to lend.
That someone is somewhere deep within.
As if a secret twin.
We have those persons deep on the inside you see.
It’s I, myself and me.

THE SILENCE IN ME

As the sun drifted across the evening sky,
I felt the need to cry.
There's so much my heart wants to say ....
But that won't chase the tears away.
Sorrows and heart aches they took my voice.
I kept it all inside me I had no choice.
My inner voice was all I could hear,
I tried to listen with tender care.
Only sobbing and sighs in between.
Lost my crown, no longer a Queen.
Inhumane silence in a quick sand of care.
There was no love for me anywhere.
My voice was drowned in deep blue of the night,
I held my heart ever so tight.
The silence in me told me all I needed to say.
This silence, guides me on my way.
The silence in me makes me brave and strong.
The silence in me keeps me from wrong.
My heart now races across the evening sky,
Because there is silence in me, I have no need to cry.

THE ATTIC

I stumbled upon myself
In the dark attic of my soul.
Cobwebs and old boxes have I uncovered.
The musty smell of old memories becoming more agile.
There, in the lonely corners of my soul, I crouch …
But the silence becomes too loud for me to bear.
I needed to escape from myself.
Tears have stained the attic floors.
Intricate pieces of my life rusted,
And lost its value.
Thoughts of death and me dancing in the twilight now
Occupy my loneliness.
I will embrace him for he beckons to me.
I'll take his hand now, as he guides me on my way, till I am ...no more.

THE EXCAVATE

With precision he tore into my soul.
Nothing was said but with brevity his words knew their place.
With hypnotic stare, broke the shackles around my will and
Drew me into him.
It was my resolve to get to a higher plane,
Where floods of indecision could not reach,
But his lips tore into my will rendering me helpless and I was
Trapped.
His tongue, excavating all that's within.
In all probity, I wanted what he had to give.
With sniper like abilities, assassinating my will.
I hung on the cliff ready to fall.
Reverting to my ancestors, a slave to their masters.
His troublesome stares,
The way he bit his lips,
Oh the way his body shimmered in the darkened light of the room.
I afforded a simper when he called my name.
His tongue finding its way to landmarks of my body, my soul.
He was the tour guide and I a tourist,
Being wowed by places he found with no diffidence
Whatsoever.
His potter like abilities moulding me in shapes,
A mathematician's envy.
In wantonness peeling away layers of me.
Opening doors shut since creation.
His eyes affixed a stare that rendered my body helpless to resist, flagrantly violating my will.
My heart unbounded but my body in shackles being willingly sacrificed for a greater good.
I was trapped as his tongue tortured my will...And I liked it.

THE ASCENT

As I stand to sit, to reminisce
What tragedy, lost melody.
I come to go how far you know
Mistakes so grand please understand.
As I rise to fall, both great and small,
All fools they are of tribal wars.
Yet I bare the shame of foolish names.
I’m up and down won't make a sound.
As I remember to forget all vain regret,
I’m awake in sleep won't make a peep.
Of heated ice, I will not splice
Yet still I rise, no compromise.
As I love to hate, won't relegate.
Where greatness is found,
Where grace abounds.
It’s my weakness to be strong,
To greatness I belong.
As I sit to stand, then take my hand.

SOUL SURGERY

Come over here baby,
Let me squeeze your stiff nipples and twirl them
With my tongue.
Your neck is as sweet as the sounds you make,
When I bite into you and release my venomous love potion
While being the antidote of your soul.
Grab my ass as I vibrate to cause an eruption.
I want to make you as hot as you make me.
Your skin like the cedars of Lebanon,
The manly scent you possess all work for a greater good in me.
I traverse my fingers through your hair.
Colours are fadeless when we kiss.
I drink you, your saliva invading me like a secret weapon.
To search the very corners of my veins, my soul.
To infiltrate my being with only desires for you.
So helpless I stand, a slave to all I hold dear. A slave to you.
Tis my sentence of servitude to a heart that holds me captive,
Dancing to only the music you play.
To the rhythm of your heart,
A symphony of our souls.

NEW YOU

With a blaze you took a torch to my soul,
Lighting every crevice making me whole.
Said all the right things, your words still lingers.
You knew all the right places to put your fingers.
Eyes are so beautifully brown,
I melted in your arms couldn't make a sound.
You engulf me like large waves rushing to the seashore.
Oh, how I need you more and more.
You are the captain so heroic and brave,
To be in your life forever is what I do crave.

IN MY EYES

Look in through this window and tell me what you see.
The eyes are a window to your soul.
You'll see in the inner parts of me.
I'm naked and vulnerable,
I'm full of surprise.
All this you'll see with a look into my eyes.
Looking in these eyes isn't for the faint of heart.
Like bright beams on a dark day,
They'll search your every part.
Through hills and valleys you go to hide your truth,
Yet these eyes of mine will often recruit…
Your very own soul to whisper and not lie,
Telling every secret sins, every time you cry.
I've happened upon a truth or two,
You might think I never had a clue.
When you at me a glance did trade,
Through your emotions my eyes did wade.
They spoke all the words you could not say.
I was the predator and you the prey.
Let my eyes witness the journey of your soul.
Through unressurected feelings let me scroll.
I'll use my eyes as the wagon on which you'll ride,
Come let me take me on the other side,
Of yourself to enter a place inside of you you've never been.
Show you undiluted sins.
These eyes of mine will always find the window to your soul,
Searching your deep emotions
Wanting to make you whole.
Unearthing all without compromise,
When you look into my eyes.

INSIDE MYSELF

I find a place inside myself
Where valleys aren't deep and mountains aren't high.
Corners are straights and doves don’t fly.
I find a place inside myself where broken dreams come through.
Goals are attainable,
There’s no one in the world but you.
I find a place inside myself
Where forest trees are abased.
The ocean is a pond,
Where… with you I belong.
I find a place inside myself,
Where you are me and I am you.
No greys only marvellous blues.
No hearts on any shelf…
No, not in this place inside myself.

FINGERS ON MY SKIN

Many things happening on the inside of me.
As I close my eyes they're like branches of a tree.
Trying to touch that one single thought,
That has to me these feelings brought.
I can feel them like fingers on my skin.
I can feel them from somewhere deep within.
They are there but not pronounced,
Just waiting on my feelings to announce.
All that's buried deep within, touching like fingers on my skin.
Am I sad, lonely? I wonder, am I blue?
Navigating these feelings without a clue.
I'm at the helm, saying, "I'm in charge."
Yet all these feelings are a mirage.
Don't know if I'm up or down, or sideways.
Can't be like this for the rest of my days.
Like fire in my soul,
Just wanting to make me whole.
Yet shall I find that single spark,
To ignite that hidden part.
Filled with greatness so bold
From days of old.
I'm being soothed from somewhere deep within
Like fingers on my… skin.
Nudging me to greatness of a higher place,
Keeping me a runner in this race... Of life.
In the midst of pain or strife.
I'm the captain of this ship.
Come let's take a trip,
And some tragedies flip,
Loosen grip,
On my shoulders no chip.
On toes of greatness let us tip,
To flip the script.

Searching deep within,
Like fingers on my skin.

BE SAFE

Be safe with me, share with me.
I'll hold a space for you
To tell me what you're going through.
I'll listen, I'll wait, I won't but in.
You can express even your deepest sins.
You are my man, my lion.
Yours were the shoulders I could cry on.
You are a man on whom I can depend.
Ever I needed it, my honour you'd defend.
I like the things you do for me.
Small things that make me quite happy.
Listening to the day I had,
Whether it was good or bad.
Opening the door of the car for me.
Sending me roses, maybe two or three.
I accept you the way you are.
Your imperfections, for leaving the fridge ajar.
I'm no walk in the park either but you made me a true believer.
So in accepting me I'll always accept you.
We've become one no longer two.
You are my thunder, my lightning, this is so true.
I believe there's nothing you can't do.
For being so brave I give you a kiss,
Oh my baby you got this.

BLUE FLAME

I'm a blue flame so deep and bright.
All of your senses to ignite.
With a passion of fire,
Igniting your desire.
With words so deep,
Sweeping you off your feet.
I'm a blue flame provoking your inner man.
Trying to make you understand.
Like fire and ice,
Quite often to splice.
A mix of the two,
That's all me, oh yes its true.
I'm a blue flame again and again.
Let there be fires of rain,
Pouring out without measure.
Finding out the treasure
That lies in my soul,
Always, to make me whole.
I'm a blue flame with soul on fire,
With a bold in me no one can hire.
So I will employ,
Life to enjoy.
In the heat of it all,
The blue deep so tall.
Flame in my eyes reaching for the stars.
Leaving everything behind, shaking off the scars.
Passion burning, making steps higher.
Blue depths of yearning, lighting me on fire.
I'm at the bottom of the sea,
With depths as deep as can be,
But all that I need still remains,
In me I'll fire up the flame.

A SMILE

A smile so soft and freely given,
A smile makes life worth the living.
A smile to take the clouds away,
A smile to brighten up the day.
A smile to show how much you care.
A smile for only you my dear.
A smile can be worth the while,
All this you do with just...
One smile.

ABOUT THE AUTHOR

Michelle Walker is a mother of five (5) beautiful children, Talena, Ashanti and Devonti who are twins, Nahjier and Nahjei, also twins. Her children are her greatest support.

She is a driver for the bus company Jamaica Urban Transit Company and she loves listening to and playing music.
She is an intermediate self-taught guitarist and song writer who enjoys dancing too. Her mantra is **"Better late than never".** She is a strong believer in human rights.
She confesses that God is her father and has never left her side and that she owes all to Him.
She is fluent in sign language and loves to spend her free time conversing with the hearing impaired.

www.ingramcontent.com/pod-product-compliance
Lightning Source LLC
LaVergne TN
LVHW010104110826
845155LV00028B/472